I HAVE FAITH
I HAVE WORKS

Elizabeth Mozell

ISBN 978-1-64299-278-6 (paperback)
ISBN 978-1-64299-279-3 (digital)

Christian Faith Publishing, Inc.
832 Park Avenue
Meadville, PA 16335
www.christianfaithpublishing.com

Printed in the United States of America

Special thanks to

Elizabeth E Ricks-Okolo for helping me with
this book, as the development editor

Introduction

Dear Reader,

Thank you for taking the time to read this *I Have Faith I Have Works* guidebook. It is a guide for anyone wanting to live their goals and dreams, a guide not a guarantee of success but a book that gives examples of how to achieve different goals big or small.

I Have Faith I Have Works takes the values of the Christian belief and translates it into achieving life's goals. A guidebook based on the author's life experiences, as she strives to achieve her personal goals of starting a business, becoming debt-free, a motivational speaker, fitness trainer, and fitness model. As she experiences different setbacks to her achievements, so will the reader. This guidebook is written when the author Elizabeth Mozell is undiscovered but working toward her dreams.

Each person who reads this book will be able to relate with trying to get out of debt, start college, a new career, and a new company, buying a car and a house, or even moving out to start over. These goals are obtainable but knowing how is the question. A good example is when college students graduate and their company internship did not hire them, what should they do? Most jobs in their field of study requires at least two years of experience in the field. Another example is if a person wants to buy a house or get out of debt, what should they do? Who can they talk to? What are the first steps?

I Have Faith I Have Works is a book that will help those who do not know how to begin walking toward their goals and dreams. This book is based on real-life events that happened to Elizabeth Mozell.

Knowing Your Life's Call

Defining our purpose in life gives us meaning to our lives. Do you remember when you were a little child when teachers would ask or tell you to draw a picture of what you wanted to be when you grow up? Most of us would say a firefighter, police officer, teacher, or even like my mom or dad. As we became older, life decisions changed, and we now had to decide what school electives we should take to set us on the right career path. The next STEP is either a good job or further our education with a specialized certificate, an associates, bachelors, masters, PhD, or doctorates. Well, in my case, the choices were college or military, two places you go to learn about the career of your choice.

College students pick a major and/or minor they feel is the right choice but realize they went to school for a hobby and not a career. People decide on a career based on what they enjoy doing. They enjoy performing a particular task but not enough to perform it all day and every day for the next twenty-five years. The outcome is "feeling stuck" while regretting their career choice or choose to go back to school.

Now the big question is, how do you identify the calling upon your life? Some may take years to define their purpose and others recognize their purpose at childhood. It is important to remember everyone is different and have different callings. Not everyone wants to be the commander and chief. Do not let anyone or any situation change your mind when you realize what is your calling.

When you wake up every morning and all you can think about is singing, dancing, cooking, fixing things, being a mentor, debating, teaching, preaching, writing, etc., then that is your calling. You may be the one with those woody ideas and inventions, then you are an inventor. No one can tell you otherwise when you learn how to trust the God in you. Having the ability to identify your calling is knowing your worth, having confidence in what you have to offer, and allowing yourself to trust the God in you that whatever you was created for will be accomplished. You are the only one that can tell anyone what you want out of life.

Who Surrounds You

Once you find out your calling, then you should surround yourself with like-minded individuals. Having friends to motivate you to keep you on the right path is very important. Now, please do not confuse the notion of only surrounding yourself with people who desire what you want to do in a career. Surrounding yourself with like-minded people is to have friends with the same drive, motivation, and determination to be successful.

The saying "birds of a feather flock together" is very true. People who are similar and have the same interest tend to form a friendship. Having friends who want your success in everything you put your hands to will greatly benefit you. Friends like this will hold you accountable, help your creativity, and give fresh ideas on a situation.

However, there are pros and cons of having friends that want you to succeed. The cons are sometimes there will heated debates about which steps you should take to get you from point A to point B. Friends and family will always have an opinion on what steps you should take, but remember, only you know what is best for you. Sometimes, friends are distractions that may hinder your dream. The pros are they will support, motivate, and keep you grounded through the good and bad times.

I asked someone, "Who do you network with? How will they invest in their future?" This person did not understand the question and became mad at me. Today I ask you, "Who do you surround yourself with? Who do you want to network with? What are you doing to achieve your goals?" Surround yourself with people who can help push you toward your dream. Sometimes, you may have to let your old friends go if they are not on the path to your success. Dead weights will only weigh you down. I have a friend I can count on to have a friendly but heated debate with me. He states his opinion and gives me unwanted information and I do the same with him. It's because we want each other to perform at our best and present the world with excellence at whatever we do. These types of friends support you in your career and will be an all-around good supporting friend in all occasions.

Networking and Connections

Networking and connections is how one expands their business, knowledge, and partnership relations. Networking and connections are two different things but have similar meanings. Networking is when a group of individuals work together to provide information, a service, or business opportunity to enhance ones career. Networking turns into contacts. Connections, on the other hand, is working alongside a particular person or group with the gathered information and contacts. Networking and connections both have a give-and-take principle, how can we BOTH benefit from each other.

Now, it is important not to only network with people to see what they can do for you but to establish relationships. Forming a friendship is the most important step when networking and making connections, especially when trying to make a name for yourself.

The best time to start networking is while you are in college. Think about it. A student may need help with a project, while another student may need experience to build their portfolio. Just about every college have an exit portfolio show. Networking while in college is more economical than going to a professional company because you get to freely use state of the art equipment as long as you properly sign it out. So, why not take advantage of the equipment and solicited instructor's help?

I had the opportunity to collaborate with a student photographer, which was a requirement for student photographers to network with the Culinary Arts students. These students needed to build their portfolios, while the Culinary Arts students saw how much work it took creating a cookbook. The young lady I was assigned to did a photoshoot of me, the food I cooked and put on plates. I told her the name and colors of the book. Today, I have my unpublish cookbook named *The Little Big Taste*. At the end of the day, everyone who came out to watch me get photoshoot and cook received free food. It was a fabulous learning experience.

Now, the next story is about how a group of students refused to network with other student clubs and break their ways of being one big clique. They did not accomplish their goal of having a Family Fun Day, which eventually was pushed back another year. I was a part of this program, so I knew firsthand how these individuals thought. If you were not a part of their program, they would not associate with you. One school day, my instructor informed the class she wanted us to host a Family Fun Day to gain community service hours that will go toward our club. Planning any type of event, with a compressed school schedule, is the most difficult thing to do. You have to maintain good grades and try to squeeze in meetings to discuss the event. Truthfully, most meetings consist of discussing the same topics for a few months because of needing to go through a proper chain of command. A few students put time toward this event by communicating with the proper people. Besides communicating, what does hosting an event consist of?

- **Brain storming**
- **Choosing a date and time**
- **Location**
- **Open to public or just students and faculty**
- **Food and drinks**
- **Music**
- **Games and prizes**
- **Sponsorship**
- **Raising money**
- **Shelter**
- **Possibility of rain? What happens?**
- **Brochures and posters**

Now looking at this list requires delegation of work and networking with others, right?

I gave a suggestion to reach out to other clubs and have the Culinary Arts Club provide the food. Having food served outside requires knowledge of the temper danger zone, time, proper cooling, and holding of the food. The Culinary Arts Club is a group of educated students who are supervised by a certified chef instructor.

Concerning the music, I reached out to the Society of Broadcaster, who provided the music with a student DJ.

Making brochures and posters are presented to the Graphic Design Club and instead of letting the Culinary program take responsibility for the food, the idea was shut down because everyone thought having food would be a hassle. The music was locked in, but due to changing of the date, they did not have anyone available. A fellow classmate did the brochure. All the effort that went into the brochure was a waste because the students thought it was too much work with having school assignments. Only if the students were open minded in collaborating the event, that would have been a success.

Every school club needs a certain number of hours and have the exposure for their school club. I even reached out to the semi-pro football team. It was all set, but I also felt the need to reach out to other people.

Networking and connections are not only for college students but for the young or older person. It is important to get to know someone because every encounter is an informative session. You can learn from a younger or older person since everyone has knowledge or an experience to share. You are never too old to learn.

There are multiple ways to network and make connections like different community events, leadership conferences, and social media. Yes! Social media is a good way to meet people with different talents who may or may not live in your area. People use social media to blog, for entertainment, and to join a common interest meet up group, which sets the foundation for a future friendship or connection. Another way to network is using webinars, conference calls, and communicating with people in general.

I admire people who do network marketing. Most people think of this industry as a pyramid scheme, but not every company is a scheme. Just to name a few, Avon and Mary Kay. Most people in this industry do not mind learning from each other. They take a no answer as NOT RIGHT NOW or "I don't want to join" as maybe you can use some of our products or services or tell a friend who may be interested in this industry. Remember, to have an open mind when meeting someone. You can network with anyone if you keep an open mind.

Visualizing the Vision

It is said, if your dreams do not scare you, then you are not dreaming big enough. Visualizing the vision and writing the vision goes hand and hand. When you visualize the vision, you start researching the how to. Before you can do something, you must understand what you are trying to do and ask yourself *why*. The *why* is the most important part. If your *why* does not show passion or make others cry, then your *why* is not strong enough.

It is good to be able to see your vison instead of only having it in your head. There are a few ways to take what is inside your mind and bring it to eye view or visualization. I recommend writing it out or drawing it. You can also be creative and make a prototype, create a vision board, or practice your talent. When I went to Culinary Art School, I created a small prototype restaurant made from small boxes and glued it onto a blue poster board. I kept that restaurant until my family and I moved, and someone threw it away while I was at school. So, I drew another restaurant on computer paper, which kept until this day. However, I do not want a restaurant but rather a café in my health and wellness fitness center.

In 2013, I went through a depression after a bad breakup. While attending a college class, I was assigned a project and it was a self-contract. This self-contract enabled me to refocus my vision as being a personal trainer and fitness model. This contract allowed me to achieve small goals working towards my dream. I wrote down a goal, in one week, I would book my first photo shoot. After completing that class assignment, I had tunnel vision towards my dream.

In 2014, I heard about Vision Boards for the first time. I made three different visions for my company. Each board represented a different department of my business. I made a Vision Board for myself and what I wanted to achieve in my personal life. It is best to start with goals that is achievable and then work towards goals that take more time to achieve. I cut out pictures of a graduation gown, a personal trainer certificate, a building to represent my fitness center, and different organizations to connect with. When you are visualizing the vision, start with goals that are achievable and work your way up to more challenging steps.

Write the Vision

I was once told to keep a pen and paper by the side of my bed to write down all my ideas. Ideas come to me when I am sleep. Writing this very book came to me at night during the month of June 2015. One day, I went to a church in Georgia with my older cousin, and the pastor preached from the book of Habakkuk 2:1–3 KJV (King James Version), "I will stand upon my watch, and set me upon the tower, and will watch to see what he will say unto me, and what I shall answer when I am reproved. And the Lord answered me, and said, Write the vision, and make it plain upon tables, that he may run that readeth it. For the vision is yet for an appointed time, but at the end it shall speak, and not lie: though it tarry, wait for it; because it will surely come, it will not tarry." After that sermon, I had a new perspective and understanding on *Write The Vision*. So, I wrote everything down in detail and sketched all my ideas. I even went as far as designing a mini building of my dream restaurant. Then, I started making vision boards of all my desired accomplishments and travel destinations.

During high school, I took business classes on Entrepreneurship, where I learned how to write a business plan. I then realized the same way the pastor preached a sermon about *Write The Vision* is the same way the bank requires you to write a business plan. What is a business plan? It is a detailed breakdown of your vision. Who are the founders? Where will it be located? Hours of operation? What is your mission statement? Financial statement analysis? These are just a few questions to answer in creating a business plan.

Normally, during your senior year of college, you have a capstone class. Capstone classes allow you to bring to life a business you worked on since your freshman year.

If the college required you to create your vision and the bank required you to write a business plan, then my question is, "How detailed will you make your vision, if it is not required?"

Write Your Vision

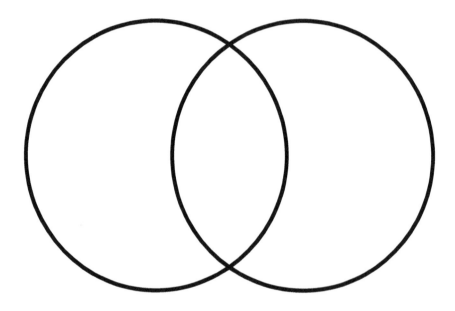

Write Your Vision

_____
_____
_____
_____
_____
_____
_____
_____
_____
_____
_____
_____
_____

Write Your Vision

_____

_____

_____

_____

_____

_____

_____

_____

_____

_____

_____

_____

Investing

Question? When is it too early to start a cash reserve? When is it too early to start investing in a 401k? When is it too early to fund a Roth IRA or mutual account? When is it okay to start thinking about early retirement? At what age should you start planning for your retirement party? When is it too early to start investing in your career? When is it too early to put money aside to invest in the things you want most?

We all have had people invest in us. This world is full of investors. These investors are underrated and underpaid compared to others. The impact they have on the world goes unnoticed. Who am I referring to? Who are these investors? Teachers. Yes, teachers are the biggest investors nest to most parents. The all investments are monetary. Time and teaching is a form of investing. Sometimes teachers are guardian angels to some kids being the only investor a child have at times. Teachers does not teach for the money but to make a difference in our children lives. Investing in one's dreams or other people visions does mean giving money all the time.

My uncle gave me my first $100.00 as an investment because I graduated high school and got accepted to college. Over the years, I have put more money into my dreams and have nothing to show for it as I write this book. My first investment was investing in a Roth IRA account and opening a checking and a savings at the age of sixteen. My next investment was attending college not once but twice. The first college was a private college, which cost most of my loan debt of $66,000.00.

In 2009, I was in a five car accident and with the settlement money I decided to invest in one of my ideas. Well, no one decided to buy my idea, so that money went down the drain, Right? No, I took a chance on my dream. With my tax return money, instead of buying clothes, shoes, or a car, I decided to attend a modeling school. Now after attending those classes, I was rejected because I am only 4'9.5 and cannot sing. I wanted to do fitness, athletic, and motivational speaking, and so I auditioned for the same company before attending the professional classes. Well, the talent scout said she did not see any talent in me. Did I take this as a setback? No! I realized not everyone will accept me and I understand I am not the average height but I will be the first to defy all the rules.

Now, I invested in two companies that most people view as a pyramid scheme, network marketing, and social Media. I also understood how regular jobs can be viewed as a pyramid having the CEO at the top, managers next, supervisors to follow, and hourly workers at the bottom.

SICK OF YOUR **J.O.B** YET?
- **Just Over Broke**
- **Juggling Our Bills**
Every J.O.B is designed to keep you dependent

Did you sign up for the 40-40-40?
1.) Work 40 Hours a Week
2.) Do That For 40 Years
3.) Retire on 40% of what
you struggled to live on
all your life
97% of Americans are stuck in a "Rat Race"

The network marketing company I connected with made excellent money. So, I decided to participate in a new social media company. The idea sounded great because it was a new website proclaiming to be better than Facebook. However, I signed up only with promises of a website that was to go public soon and a year later it is still private. So, why did I choose to leave network marketing and social media? I left the social media because I realized it was not for me. This company does have a social website that is similar to Facebook, but I am not comfortable signing up people with only promises of *one day*. If this company ever surpass Facebook and become the next big website, then I missed the boat. I do remember how Myspace was the number one social media site and then came Facebook. This is a chance I am willing to take.

As for the network marketing company, I decided to put it on pause to chase my dreams. Most people will get caught up into making fast money and put their dreams on hold. Representative of network marketing and social media talk of retiring early, making it big, and extra income. However, without hard work, dedication, and self-motivation, it will not work. People want that overnight success but fail to realize it is just a myth. Overnight success rarely happens.

In network marketing they say becoming a representative is a good way to raise funding for your different goals and dreams you want to achieve. However, I witnessed many individuals who placed their dream on hold to peruse network marketing. Eventually their dream is on hold for months, which turns into years. To get any success you must work the company like a full-time job. The idea of working network marketing only for two hours out the day sounds great but that is the minimum to just to build your team. To achieve great success, you must put more time in building your team than two hours. My perspective about network marketing is, it is an implanted goal not your actual goal you wanted to achieve. An implanted goal is a goal or dream someone else introduced to you. The person being introduced to the companying did not wake up saying that's what I want to achieve in life, but rather seen a presentation of a network marketing company. An actual goal is a goal a person wakes up daily wanting to achieve.

I decided to start my second major of study at a community college that required me to take a yearlong compressed schedule. The school compressed their classes from a fourteen-week to a seven-week school term. So, I had to go from working full time to part time and give up any form of social life. Through the short time I have lived, I realized many individuals are not willing to give up their social life for school. Why? As for me, I placed my social life and network marketing on hold for school. No, I do not regret my decision. I chose not to be the one who ran after money but ran after my dreams. I am enjoying the process as my dreams unfold. As I write this book, I believe millions and millions of people will read this. I am not rich nor do I have all the answers, but I am investing time, money, and effort in this book.

The world is a pyramid complex itself.

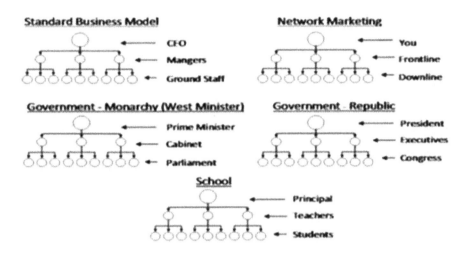

Work Your Faith

Nike said it best, *Just Do It*. You must be the first to believe in yourself. You have to be the one to take the first step in achieving your dreams. In James 2:14–18 NKJV (New King James Version), it says, "What does it profit, my brethren, if someone says he has faith but does not have works? Can faith save him? If a brother or sister is naked and destitute of daily food, and one of you says to them, 'Depart in peace, be warmed and filled,' but you do not give them the things which are needed for the body, what does it profit? Thus also faith by itself, if it does not have works, is dead. But someone will say, *You have faith, and I have works*. Show me your faith without your *works*, and I will show you my faith by my *works*."

This particular text gives an example of meeting a person in need of clothes, food, and shelter, who was spoken poorly of and their needs were not met. You can use this Bible verse and apply it to whatever you want to achieve. You cannot only talk about your dream, but you have to put actions behind your words. How do you work your faith?

Prerequisites: Before you can take action, you must first be knowledgeable of how to achieve your dream.

- **Do the research about what you want to achieve.**
- **Attend different workshops, classes, and seminars.**
- **Read books.**
- **Do internships and informative interviews.**
- **Capstone: It consists of research and the development of a major product or project that is an extension of the research.**
- **Create a business plan.**
- **Create a website or use social media.**
- **Continue to educate yourself.**
- **Change the way you think.**
- **Be the first to part take in what you want.**
- **Nike *Just Do It*… Create your own opening.**
- **Start small in a garage, apartment, and basement.**
- **Build clientele (start with yourself).**
- **Invest (time, money, and then investors).**

I believe in leading by example. I named this book *I Have Faith I Have Works* after reading James chapter 2. I would talk about how I wanted to do this and that and never put action behind my words. Actions speak louder than words.

Once I realized I needed actions, I became full force and used part of my tax money to go back to modeling school. I enrolled back in school to become a personal trainer and attend different seminars and workshops. I keep up with the latest trends in health, nutrition, and sports. Also, to keep my certification, I have to take different classes.

I created a business plan and built my clientele with me being the first client. I continue to work full time at a hospital as startup investment. I hate my job, but the big picture is that it helps fund my business as I search for a job in my area of study to gain experience. I am writing this book believing I will be able to help my readers.

Branding

On December 27, 2014, I scheduled a photoshoot for my birthday, but little did I know I would encounter someone who would change my life. After the photoshoot, I met a model who modeled for TAP, he gave me words of wisdom. He told me to create my own buzz and build my own fan base. If no one is willing to give you an opportunity, then create an opportunity for yourself. *In other words, make your own entrance if no one wants to open the door and let you in.*

Today is the Age of Technology. You have everything at your fingertips. It is easy to build a fan base using social media such as YouTube, Facebook, Instagram, Snapchat, Twitter, and Blogging. Do not be afraid to use social media as a way to brand and market yourself, instead of using it as an outlet to vent about different things.

When the underwear model gave me these instructions, I created a YouTube page and a Facebook page under the name Elizabeth Mozell. I uploaded motivational and inspirational videos and videos of my workouts. I created a website to inform the world who is Elizabeth Mozell, elizabethmozell.webs.com. Since then I have created another website alphafittsports.com.

My question is to you, *How are you utilizing your access opportunities?* Different ways to start branding yourself are as follows: Network with those who believe what you believe, write blogs, upload videos to YouTube, Periscope, and create a Facebook and company page. Step out of your comfort zone and talk to people. Use all social media of your choice and change your attitude (I think, therefore I am) Descartes, René.

Photo Credit
Quintin Hazelton
Millionaire Mentality

Photo Credit
Terrance A Morgan
Terrance Antonio Photography
TAP

Photo Credit
Terrance A Morgan
Terrance Antonio Photography
TAP

Photo Credit
Keith Henderson

Photo Credit
Terrance A Morgan
Terrance Antonio Photography
TAP

Doubting Thomas

Please, let me be the first to say this if you haven't heard, your parents and friends may say they believe in you, but if you ask for support for you and your dream, they just may be *lookers*. *Lookers* are people who say they believe in you and your dream but only watch to see if you make it or fail. It is not because they do not want you to be successful but because your dream is so big, it is hard for them to see your vision on the scale you are describing to them. They know your history and upbringings. There is a Bible verse that says this, Mark 6:4 (KJV, King James Version), "But Jesus to them, A prophet is not without honor except in his own country, among his own kin, and in his own house." Strangers will be the first to believe in you before your family and friends.

Be careful who you tell your dream to big or small. There are people who would like to take your idea and then there are those who would like to doubt you and talk behind your back. I know this all so well. First, when I started network marketing, my family thought it was a pyramid scheme. I went through three different companies but only one would work.

When I started training and building my company, a few of my family members were sarcastically asking (with a smirk on their faces), what happened to this or that? Are you still doing this and that? All they knew is I worked a full time job but did not know I trained before or after work.

So excited about becoming a fitness model, I would show pictures to coworkers and then over hear them say, "Oh, she must think she is really going to get her pictures in a magazine? I do not believe she is really trying but rather talking just to hear herself talk." Over hearing them made me feel hurt but determined to succeed.

Back to the Drawing Board

There is no time limit on the road to success. As time passed, I realized becoming a fitness model was not what I wanted to do but rather help people make healthy life changing decisions. Instead of self-gratification, I wanted to have a positive impact on my community and serve others. I wanted to be like the perfect servant. Who is that perfect servant you may ask? Jesus, yes Jesus. Jesus demonstrated how to serve others during the last super:

> So he got up from the meal, took off his outer clothing, and wrapped a towel around his waist. After that, he poured water into a basin and began to wash his disciples' feet, drying them with the towel that was wrapped around him. He came to Simon Peter, who said to him, "Lord, are you going to wash my feet?" Jesus replied, "You do not realize now what I am doing, but later you will understand." "No," said Peter, "You shall never wash my feet." Jesus answered, "Unless I wash you, you have no part with me." (John 13:4-8 (NIV, New International Version))

Nothing made me happy then watching those with disabilities achieve greatness through exercising. I notice in the fitness industry the disabled is underrepresented. Therefore, I established Alpha Fitness Life LLC. I started at home first. My father and I loved going to the gym together. My father is also among the disabled population having spinal injuries. I have seen firsthand how most of the equipment at the gyms are not disabled people friendly. People among this population have a hard time overcoming different obstacles in life.

Why should they have to face challenges at a place they can use as an outlet?

Alpha Fitness Life target market is the special population consisting of disabled individuals and those with various diseases. This special population is underrepresented in the fitness industry. Many gyms tend to focus on strength and conditioning, body building, and the athlete instead of focusing on everyone including the special population. Alpha Fitness Life isn't only a gym but a health and wellness center. Our focus is to cater to people's health and well-being. Our goal is to collaborate with different health and wellness and nutrition companies. These companies specialize in catering to the special population needs and wants such as the *Academy of Nutrition and Dietetics* and *Foodservice Professionals*. Alpha Fitness Life plans to offer dietary counselling and healthy cooking classes by collaborating with Register Dietitians and Dietetic Chefs.

Alpha Fitness Life is established for those among the special population who are physically disabled, who are underrepresented, and face many personal challenges. Many gyms target the athletes and body builders market and hardly represent the disabled population.

Knowledge Is Power

Having a career is perfectly acceptable. There is no rule on how many career paths one can take. Yes, you may be the "butt of the joke" at family events, but whatever makes you happy, do it as long as your career choice is your decision and not influenced by someone else. For an example, I went from becoming a certified chef working in a few restaurants, to becoming a certified personal trainer working at a hospital in dietary, just to gain a certification in sports nutrition. Those with an untrained eye will see this as a career change. However, I expanded my scope of practice in my career field. I even took a chance at network marketing. For years, people asked why did I change careers? My brother even told me numerous times, I went to school and I did not use my degree and certifications. People only think having a Culinary Arts Degree means you only work in a kitchen cooking food. With a Culinary Arts Degree, you can become a food critic, a food journalist, food photographer and a nutritionist. With my personal trainer certificate, I can offer personal training and personal chef services because diet and exercising goes hand and hand.

Do not be afraid to expand your scope of practice or change careers. What people say or think about you does not concern you or effect your life or dream. How can you focus on bettering yourself, if you are worried about what others are saying? Remember you do not owe anyone an explanation.

Even the Bible shows career changes and without the people's approval. Some even wanted to know how will the career change benefit the family.

In Matthew 4:18–22, (NLV, New Life Version), Jesus calls Peter and Andrew,

Jesus was walking by the Sea of Galilee. He saw two brothers.

They were Simon (his other name was Peter) and Andrew, his brother.

They were putting a net into the sea for they were fishermen.

Jesus said to them, "Follow Me. I will make you fish for men!"

At once they left their nets and followed Him.

Going from there, Jesus saw two other brothers. They were James and John, the sons of Zebedee. They were sitting in a boat with their father, mending their nets. Jesus called them. At once they left the boat and their father and followed Jesus.

In Matthew 20:20–22, (NLV, New Life Version), the mother of James and John asks Jesus a tough question,

The mother of Zebedee's children (James and John) came to Jesus with her sons.

She got down on her knees before Jesus to ask something of Him. He said to her, "What do you want?" She said, "Say that my two sons may sit, one at Your right side and one at Your left side, when You are King." Jesus said to her, "You do not know what you are asking. Are you able to take the suffering that I am about to take?

Are you able to be baptized with the baptism that I am baptized with?" They said, "Yes, we are able." He said to them, "You will suffer as I will suffer. But the places at My right side and at My left side are not Mine to give. Whoever My Father says will have those places.

In Acts 9:1–2, 20–22, (NKJV, New King James Version), the Damascus Road where Saul was converted,

Then Saul, still breathing threats and murder against the disciples of the Lord, went to the high priest and asked letters from him to the synagogues of Damascus, so that if he found any who were of the Way, whether men or women, he might bring them bound to Jerusalem.

Saul Preaches Christ, v. 20–22

Immediately he preached the Christ in the synagogues, that He is the Son of God.

Then all who heard were amazed, and said, "Is this not he who destroyed those who called on this name in Jerusalem, and has come here for that purpose, so that he might bring them bound to the chief priests?" But Saul increased all the more in strength, and confounded the Jews who dwelt in Damascus, proving that this Jesus is the Christ.

In Judges 4:4 (KJV, King James Version)

"And Deborah, a prophetess, the wife of Lapidoth, she judged Israel at that time."

Esther 7: 3-4 (NKJV, New King James Verse)
Esther Saves the Jews

Then Queen Esther answered and said, "If I have found favor in your sight, O king, and if it pleases the king, let my life be given me at my petition, and my people at my request. For we have been sold, my people and I, to be destroyed, to be killed, and to be annihilated. Had we been sold as male and female slaves, I would have held my tongue, although the enemy could never compensate for the king's loss.

Esther 8:3–8 (NKJV, New King James Verse)

Now Esther spoke again to the king, fell down at his feet, and implored him with tears to counteract the evil of Haman the Agagite, and the scheme which he had devised against the Jews. And the king held out the golden scepter toward Esther. So Esther arose and stood before the king, and said, 'If it pleases the king, and if I have found favor in his sight and the thing seems right to the king and I am pleasing in his eyes, let it be written to revoke the letters devised by Haman, the son of Hammedatha the Agagite, which he wrote to annihilate the Jews who are in all the king's provinces. For how can I endure to see the evil that will come to my people? Or how can I endure to see the destruction of my countrymen?'

Then King Ahasuerus said to Queen Esther and Mordecai the Jew,

Indeed, I have given Esther the house of Haman, and they have hanged him on the gallows because he tried to lay his hand on the Jews. You yourselves write a decree concerning the Jews, as you please, in the king's name, and seal it with the king's signet ring; for whatever is writ-

ten in the king's name and sealed with the king's
signet ring no one can revoke.

Throughout the Bible, people had career change, became civil
right leaders, and saved nations. Jesus took fishermen and made them
missionaries. Paul, formally named Saul and a "zealous" Pharisee who
"intensely persecuted" the followers of Jesus, became a follower of
Jesus and preacher. Deborah was a wife, a prophetess in her church,
and a judge. She also was the Judge Judy of her day. Now Esther was
as common as you and I and she became queen by hiding her iden-
tity. Becoming queen is not what she is known for but for saving her
race from being killed. She petitioned the king to save her people.
She would be considered a civil rights leader of her time.

As I previously stated, family members and friends may criticize
or approve of the change. In modern-day language, the mother of
James and John asked Jesus how her sons would benefit from leaving
the family business to becoming missionaries? People disapproved of
Paul's career change due to his past. Paul was what you call a modern-day bounty hunter of his time. Sometimes, people will have
a hard time believing you changed and want to do good because
of who you use to be. Esther's uncle, Mordecai, encourage her to
become queen and to save her people. Even throughout the Bible,
people always approved or disapproved of change. Remember as long
as you are happy with your career change, it does not matter who
approves or disapproves.

The Process

For the longest I wanted to become a fitness model and it was not until 2014 that I wanted to own a health and wellness fitness center. I went to school to study personal training, watched videos, and read books about health and wellness. As I found my passion, I encourage all my friends to find their calling. I felt like I was making progress in my career. However, a year later, I found myself being question by one of my friends. He and I were at a restaurant in Florida, when he asked about my career. I informed him I was in the process and doing research. He proceeded to ask what was I doing to make my dream a reality? I did not realize I was stagnant for a year, not making any progress. How was the same guy I encourage to go after his dream, now encouraging me to do the same? I lost all sense of accomplishment and now my drive and my will went into over drive. I became eager to begin the journey. Alpha Fitness Life and the Alpha Fitt clothing line were in full affect.

What does Alpha Fitt mean? Why choose Alpha Fitt? The word Alpha means change, growth, success, individualism, leadership, and dominance. In the Alpha Fitt community, we believe in living life to the FULLEST through a change of lifestyle and a healthier mind, body, and spirit. Having a healthier lifestyle increases ones self-confidence, sense of achievement, and self-discipline. Alpha Fitt incorporates the FITT principle (Frequency, Intensity, Time, and Type) to help promote a healthier way of living.

Next I had to brainstorm the concept of the logo. What will the logo consist of? The name of my company is Alpha Fitness Life and the brand is Alpha Fitt. My favorite animal is the wolf, so after awhile, the logo was created. Similar to the structure in a wolf pack, there is an Alpha male and Alpha female. We, the Alpha Fitt community, are all Alpha males and Alpha females. WE ARE EQUAL, no big "I" and no little "you." Remember, I informed you to network with people you went to school with. I knew a young man from high school who made professional logos for various people. Being a fan of his work, I asked him if he could create my company's logo. Having the logo under way, I began researching organizations lending a helping hand to entrepreneurs. SCORE, Center for Women, and Charleston Young Professionals were three organizations which helped me greatly. These organizations offered business mentoring services, webinars, networking opportunities, various workshops, and one on one mentoring. I felt like the world was at my fingertips. The world became my playground with all the resources available. I don't understand why many people from Charleston, SC move out of state to start a company. There are many resources available for entrepreneurs and network opportunities and I had my hand in all three organizations. Start where you are, not where you want to be. If the resource is at your fingertips, then why not start the process? Why wait to move for the right time? For me the right time was right then and now. Talking with a mentor and attending one networking event gave me the realization I had to step up my game to play in the big leads.

I went *back to the drawing board*. I had a great idea and that's all it was. I needed help with my business plan, business cards, to figure out how to brand my company and build a team. So much to do for one person with a full-time job, with so little time but having SCORE and Center For Women help me greatly. I was to put things into focus and start a business plan while advertising via social media, Craig List, and free ads in local newspapers.

Through advertisement, multiple people had interest working for Alpha Fitness Life. However, Alpha Fitness Life was in the development phase and unable to pay. At the time, I needed individuals who would not mind volunteering until funds increased. Their e-mails to apply for the position usually began with them telling me how they are interested, and then giving me their qualifications and resume. I would reply with more details about Alpha Fitness Life. Tell my why? Lastly, I proceeded to say this will be an unpaid position until profits comes. All that interest went out the window, once they realized the position was unpaid.

There were a few individuals who came on board and was okay with volunteering; however, they did not last. One person agreed to volunteer but did not work. He made every excuse on why he could not work for Alpha Fitness. We had multiple meetings, giving him chances. He did network marketing with Legal Shield but did no work and kept showing his legal shield lawyers and mentors the business plan. During that time, I was in the process of having everything trademark. This individual gave me chills because he wanted me to create a position for his friend. Then he mentioned how his mentors advised him and suggested this and that. What really was a red flag, is when he mentioned how people can try to take the company's name and logo and then asked if I had the company trademark. I informed him I had the company and logo trademark and no one could take it. He also went on Alpha Fitness Life social media page and change the company number to his number without running it by me. I was updating the page and notice the change. Also, I sent a friend request to him on a professional social media account and he accepted my request but took his picture and information down. He created a new account that I did not have. Why would a person who refused to do any work for Alpha Fitness Life show his mentors (who are lawyers) the business plan, want me to sign on his friend to the company, and mention how people able to take the company logo if not trademark, just to delete his social media account information? Why? Two reasons, either he wanted to take the company or he wanted his name associate with Alpha Fitness Life just in case the company became a success.

The life lesson in this is be careful of those who want to steal your ideas. Always cover yourself. If you think your idea has value, then spend the money. So, many people advised me to do a poor man's trademark. A poor man's trademark is when you mail the item you want trademarked to yourself. Tape the entire package and do not open it once mailed, thus creating a time mark for yourself. Therefore, if anyone claims they had the idea or used the logo first, you have a time and date from the post office. I can only imagine how things would have turned out, if I had used the poor man's trademark. That guy may have taken my company's name and logo. I met my patent attorney at one of SCORE's inventors meeting. I had the opportunity ask him questions about different topics. I am glad I spent the money. The second life lesson is be aware of those who want to attach themselves to you. If they do not benefit you or put forth effort in accomplishing your dreams, then consider them leeches.

Logo Credit:
Bill Simmons

Figure 1 first logo attempt

Logo Credit:
Bill Simmons

Figure 1 final logo

For The Reader

The Journey to Discovery Continues

Life is full of adventures. I am currently writing this guidebook as I establish my company. Alpha Fitness Life LLC is still in the beginning phase. For two years, I have gained lots of support. Many people such as friends and family have offered to help. As I for stated in the previous chapter, family and friends are what you call *lookers*. Their support comes once others start supporting you. Often the most support comes through the unseen support.

I have told how the first person I signed on was not a good fit and how others agreed to work for paid and not volunteer. I understand why they turned down the opportunity. People have families to feed, working without pay, would be an irrational decision. I did not let one bad apple spoil the bunch. I continued to post ads and receive e-mails of interest. I even had a few individuals willing to work for free. However, their work schedules and schooling did not permit them to continue with Alpha Fitness Life. After all, knowledge is power. When it comes to choosing which is a priority and which is not a priority, Alpha Fitness Life was not as important as they thought.

No, I do not know when Alpha Fitness Life will reach its full potential, but I know it will happen with all the great feedback. I know for sure having more capital will help a great deal, so I continue to encourage myself, knowing the right people will come along in due time, God's time. What speaks volume; is when I became sick (finding out I was pregnant) multiple people call and message me, asking why I stopped promoting my company. I became extremely motivated.

You now know my story. I hope this book will help you strive to achieve your dream just as it pushed me towards mine.

Some of the books in which inspired me to achieve my dream are as follows:

The Holly Bible
Rich Dad Poor Dad
Rich Dad Poor Dad: Before I Quit My Job
The Power of Broke

About the Author

Elizabeth Mozell's passion for fitness is hereditary predates her birth. Before her parents found out God had blessed with children, her father and mother would exercise and play tennis together. On December 28, 1989, Elizabeth Mozell was born.

She really did not become interested in fitness until she took a JROTC class as an elective in high school and joined the JROTC's Raider Team. The Raider Team is a special force, physical training JROTC team. While on the team, Elizabeth competed in a few team competitions such as One-Mile Run, One-Mile March, and the Push-up and Sit-up test. Upon graduation from high school, she kept up the training and soon found herself giving exercise advice to others throughout the years.

Now, cooking is another passion of hers; she decided attend college and study Culinary Arts. Elizabeth Mozell received a Bachelor of Science Degree in Culinary Arts Management. She soon realized diet and exercise went hand and hand. In 2013, Elizabeth decided to attend college once again to become a fitness specialist and graduated in 2015 as an ACE Certified Personal Trainer.

Her calling in life is to help motivate and inspire those who have low self-esteem, dreams they want to achieve, and those who fear failure. Owning a health and wellness fitness center is a dream of hers and her satisfaction comes through coaching and motivating each client. In 2016 Elizabeth Mozell started her company Alpha Fitness Life.

CPSIA information can be obtained
at www.ICGtesting.com
Printed in the USA
BVHW061951140323
660406BV00024B/1364